SWIFT WALKER

A Continental Journey

Written by VERLYN TARLTON

Illustrated by ALEJANDRO CHAMBERLAIN

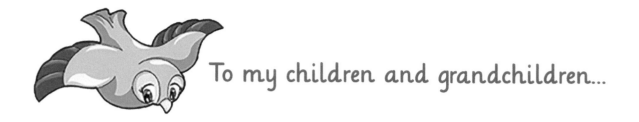

To my children and grandchildren...

Plum Street Press
A Division of Yes, MAM Creations

Published by Plum Street Press
www.PlumStreetPressBooks.com

Editing and research by **Candace E. West**
Maps by **Norma Andriani Eka Putri**

ISBN-13: 978-1-943169-10-8

SWIFT WALKER

A Continental Journey

Written by VERLYN TARLTON
Illustrated by ALEJANDRO CHAMBERLAIN

Swift Walker walked faster than everybody. Even his little dog could barely keep up with him!

His mom would say, "Slow down, Swift!"
His dad would say, "Son, you walk too fast!"
His sister would say, "One day you'll walk so fast, you won't be able to stop!"

But Swift kept right on walking.

One sunny afternoon, Swift took a walk... a fast walk, of course. After a few hours, Swift realized he was tired. He wanted to slow down, but his feet would not stop. They kept right on walking!

AFRICA!

Swift walked by...

...the Sahara Desert, the largest desert in the world. The sun shone brightly as the dry air warmed his face.

...Mt. Kilimanjaro, the highest mountain in Africa.

...the Serengeti, where he saw a herd of large African elephants.

...the beautiful Nile River, which runs from one end of Africa all the way to the other.

"Wow!" he said. "Amazing!"
But Swift's feet kept right on walking
out of Africa and straight on to...

He couldn't believe what he saw...

...the Eiffel Tower looked like it reached the sky and touched the clouds.

...St. Basil's Cathedral, the most beautiful cathedral in Europe. What a masterpiece!

...the North Cape in Norway with its peaceful waters. It looked like paradise.

"Wow!" he said. "Amazing!" But Swift's feet kept right on walking out of Europe and straight on to...

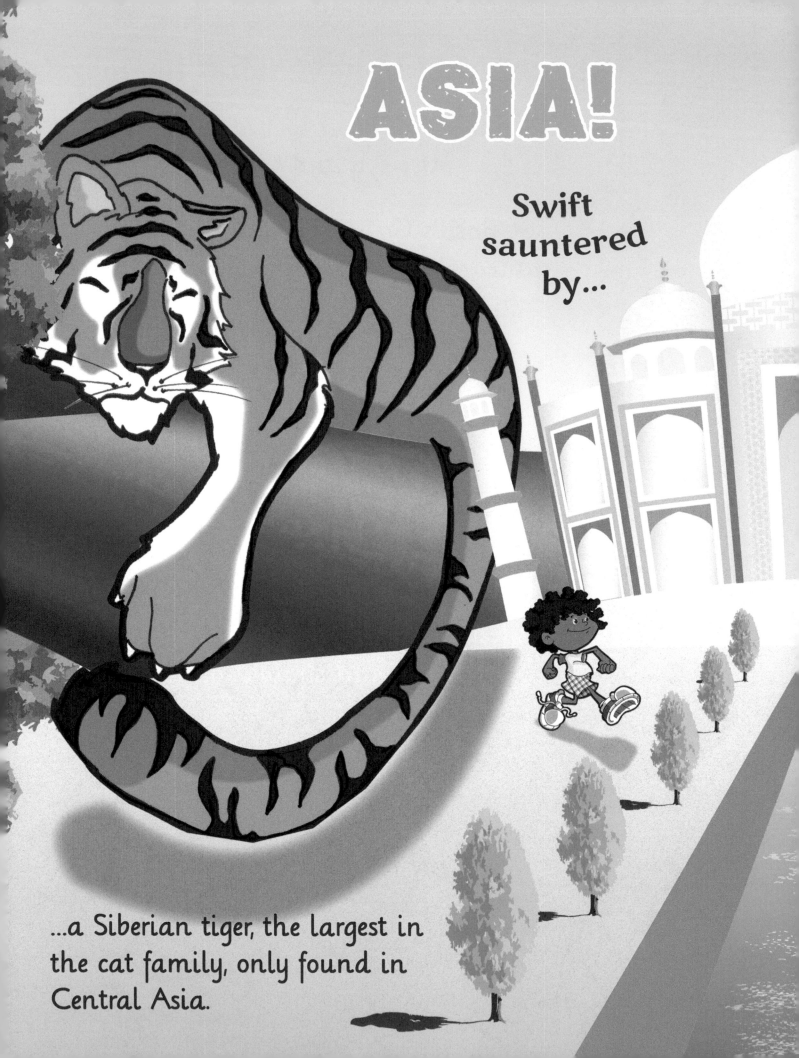

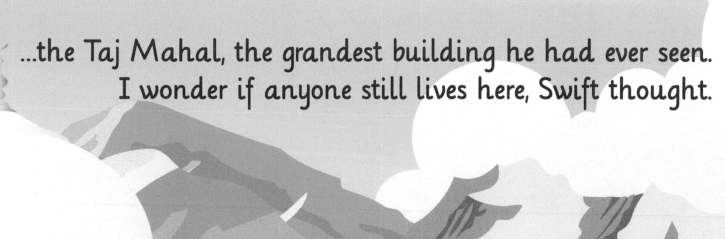

...the Taj Mahal, the grandest building he had ever seen. I wonder if anyone still lives here, Swift thought.

"Wow!" he said. "Amazing!" But Swift's feet kept right on walking out of Asia and straight on to...

...the Yangtze River, the longest river in Asia.

...the Kanangra Falls in Kanangra Boyd National Park where waters cascaded down the big rock wall.

...Koala bears eating from a fragrant eucalyptus tree.

...the Harbour Bridge and Opera House in Sydney. He could see the whole city from there!

"Wow!" he said. "Amazing!" But Swift's feet kept right on walking out of Australia and straight on to...

ANTARCTICA!

Swift
passed by...

...a mommy seal and
her pup rubbing noses.

...the slow moving rivers of ice called valley glaciers.

...Observation Hill where he saw the best view, clear across Antarctica.

"Wow!" he said. "Amazing!"
But Swift's feet kept right on walking
out of Antarctica and straight on to...

...Mount Cotopaxi in Ecuador, the world's tallest active volcano. Will it erupt soon? Swift wondered.

...the damp Amazon Rainforest and the towering BrazilNut Trees.

...a red poison tree frog whose colors are a warning to stay away!

...the Atacama Desert in Chile with the Hand of the Desert made of cement and iron.

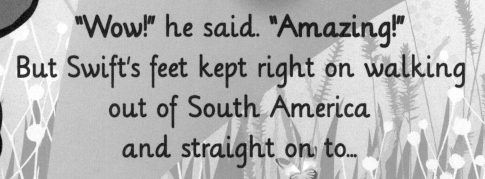

"Wow!" he said. "Amazing!" But Swift's feet kept right on walking out of South America and straight on to...

Swift spotted...

...the Spirit of Washington sailing down the Potomac River in Washington, DC, the nation's capital.

...Horseshoe Bend on the Colorado River. It looked like the bend was full of green and blue jelly!

...an enormous whale diving in the waters of the Auke Bay off the Alaska Shores.

"Wow!" he said. "Amazing!"
But Swift's feet kept right on walking until he found himself...

...in his bed.

When he looked down at his feet, Swift realized his great adventure was a dream. Or was it?

"Wow!" he said. "Amazing!"

AFRICA!

The Sahara Desert is the largest hot desert on the planet. It's almost as big as China or the United States and covers 10 different countries!

Further south, in the country of Tanzania, stands Mt. Kilimanjaro, the highest mountain on the continent.

The Nile river is the longest in the world, beginning in central Africa and flowing all the way north to the Mediterranean Sea.

The Sahara Desert

Mt. Kilimanjaro

The Nile River

ANTARCTICA!

Esperanza Base

Antarctica is the coldest continent and the largest desert on Earth. The temperature there is usually below freezing, even in the summer! Because it is so cold there, almost all of Antarctica is covered in ice.

In fact, Antarctica is so cold and so dry that no one can live there all the time. Most of the people who live there for a while are scientists. Scientists from all over the world go to Antarctica to study climate and animals like penguins, seals, and whales.

Antarctica

Emperor Penguins

ASIA!

Asia, the eastern part of the Eurasian landmass, is the largest of the 7 continents. More than half of the world's people—60% of all humans!—live in Asia.

The Taj Mahal, located in northern India, is world-famous for its beauty.

The Yangtze River runs through China, the country with the world's largest population.

Siberian tigers are also from Asia and live mainly in Russia, the largest country in the world. Sprawling across both Asia and Europe, Russia is twice the size of the Australian continent. Despite its massive size, Russia is one of the most sparsely populated countries in the world.

The Taj Mahal

The Yangtze River

Siberian Tiger

AUSTRALIA!

Great Barrier Reef

Most of Australia's population lives in the east, in cities like Sydney and Melbourne.

Australia is the smallest of the continents. In the north, sea turtles and brightly-colored tropical fish swim in the Great Barrier Reef. In the south, Kangaroo Island is home to many kinds of marsupials—kangaroos, but also koalas and wombats. Western Australia is mostly Outback—a vast desert where dingoes hunt for prey.

Outback
Uluru

Kangaroo

EUROPE!

Europe, the western part of the Eurasian landmass, is the second-smallest continent, but has the second-largest population.

In Paris, also known as The City of Lights, you can climb to the top of the Eiffel Tower and see the city sparkle below. St. Basil's Cathedral, with it's colorful domes, is in the center of Russia's capital, Moscow.

The Eiffel Tower and The River Seine

The Eiffel Tower

St. Basil's Cathedral

NORTH! AMERICA!

North America can be divided into six regions: Greenland, Canada, the United States, Mexico, Central America, and the Caribbean. Greenland and parts of Canada and Alaska are in the Arctic—the Earth's northernmost region.

Juneau, Alaska

Auke Bay can be found in Juneau, Alaska. Because of its rough terrain, there are no roads connecting Juneau to other cities in Alaska, or to the rest of North America.

Some of the coldest places in the world are in Alaska, Canada, and Greenland. But the hottest place on earth is also on the North American continent: Death Valley, California's Furnace Creek.

Death Valley

The Potomac River

In the United States, the Potomac River flows through 3 states and Washington, DC, the country's capital.

SOUTH AMERICA!

South America is the most biodiverse continent. That means that South America has more different kinds of plants and animals than any other place on Earth! One reason for this is the Amazon rainforest, which is home to 2.5 million different species of insects alone!

Mount Cotopaxi, an active volcano, is in Ecuador—named for its location at the Earth's Equator. The Equator is an imaginary line around the Earth's surface that is equidistant from the North and South Poles.

Llamas on Mt. Cotopaxi

Mt. Cotopaxi, Ecuador

Mt. Cotopaxi, Ecuador

About the Author

Verlyn Tarlton, a native Washingtonian, is a mother, wife, speaker, and author. She got her love of reading and writing from her late grandfather, Ethelbert W. Haskins, who was a university professor in Washington, DC. She has always been passionate about reading, writing, and teaching. She especially wants to pass on her love of reading and adventure to young children and encourage them to dream BIG!

www.facebook.com/verlyntarlton

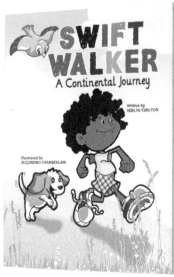

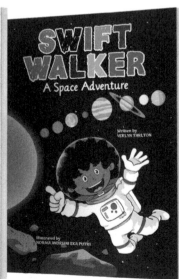

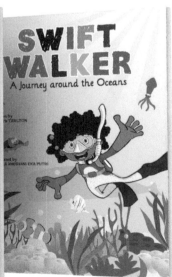